Curve Away from Stillness

John Allman

Curve Away from Stillness

Science Poems

AFTERWORD BY PETER S. COLEMAN,

NEW YORK UNIVERSITY

A NEW DIRECTIONS BOOK

Grateful acknowledgment is made to the following publications, in which some of the poems in this collection first appeared: *The Agni Review, The Beloit Poetry Journal,* and *New Directions in Prose and Poetry.*

Manufactured in the United States of America
New Directions Books are printed on acid-free paper.
First published as New Directions Paperbook 667 in 1989
Published simultaneously in Canada by Penguin Books Canada Limited

Library of Congress Cataloging-in-Publication Data

Allman, John, 1935–
    Curve away from stillness: science poems / John Allman;
afterword by Peter S. Coleman.
    p.   cm.—(New Directions paperbook; 667)
    ISBN 0-8112-1081-2 (pbk.)
    1.   Science—Poetry.
    PS3551.L46C8   1989
    811'.54—dc19
                                                    88–22791
                                                    CIP

New Directions Books are published for James Laughlin
by New Directions Publishing Corporation,
80 Eighth Avenue, New York 10011

CONTENTS

for Jennifer and the future

"Night which Pagan Theology could make the daughter of *Chaos*, affords no advantage to the description of order: Although no lower than that Masse can we derive its Genealogy. All things began in order, so shall they end, and so shall they begin again. . . ."

Sir Thomas Browne
The Garden of Cyrus

PROLEGOMENON

Connections between poetry and science: old as the ones between poetry and cosmology, beauty and knowledge, pleasure and speculation. It may only be in recent times that we separate the poetic experience from the world of measurable facts, believing that there's something so neutral, so unpretty, so abstract in the laws of the physical world, that poets must withdraw from scientific views as from harsh and prosaic metals. Why do physicists speak of elegance and symmetry in their equations? Why do scientists resort to metaphor to explain their facts? Why do both poetry and science speak of the singular and the universal?

Valéry: "*What is of value for one person only has no value. This is the iron law of Literature.*"[1] And of science.

Poetry must be personal. It verifies our subjective existence. It is the living nerve between in-here and out-there. But it also creates what Sir Philip Sidney called the "speaking picture" that the study of history, by itself, cannot provide; and that science, by itself, would be too blind to see, for facts and theories are not always visions, not syntheses, though scientific data—the observed *things*—are rich with the physical beginnings of metaphor. That "things" can stand apart from an unprejudiced perception is a myth that has fallen, as has the claim for the objective character of scientific method. That something can be unchangingly *there* conflicts with Heisenberg's uncertainty principle in quantum theory, which Einstein was unable to rebuff. A particle is merely a "wave of probabilities," a state of being that "collapses into definite form only when it is actually observed."[2] There is no simple, stable, unfluctuating, metrical reality. There is ambiguity. There is an average presence, typical behavior, relationship. There is perpetual tendency, an always dis-

[1]Paul Valéry, "Poetry and Abstract Thought" (tr. Denise Folliot), p. 160, in *Paul Valéry: An Anthology*, ed. James R. Lawler, Princeton University Press, 1977.

[2]Malcolm W. Browne, *The New York Times*, February 11, 1986.

appearing present. In observation, we create ourselves around the core of something we say is external. In poetry, releasing the seen from Coleridge's flow of the Primary Imagination.

Both poetry and science, in every era, drag myths along. Lucretius could not give up the gods in *De Rerum Natura*. Newtonian mechanics led to the ether as a medium for "forces": repudiated after Einstein understood the Michaelson/Morley experiments with light. What Einstein said was impossible—that anything could travel faster than the speed of light: now challenged by Alan Guth's theory that the universe inflated exponentially before the big bang (also described as cosmic repulsion, involving the concept of antigravity that Einstein denied). And matter being created at the event horizon of a black hole—a world created out of the void. The Book of Genesis in its way, correct. All myths true, as embroidered coats are.

Scientific ideas, beliefs, metaphors form an ambient philosophy of matter: a commonalty not to be found in politics or religious fundamentalism. Not that science is new to poetry, but that it is pervasive in metaphoric constructions. That it is at once the ground of agreement and disagreement, where imaginings are continually generated, even as history records the conflicts of new life and old forms. What Eliot called the simultaneous order of all art, his sense of a tradition, is increasingly represented not by art but by science. Students learn about DNA and quantum leaps before reading Sappho, Dante, Rilke.

The poem as the mind acting—theorizing, remembering, and most of all: making. In this book, unpunctuated meditations and narratives using the white space of the page as a unit of breath and rhythm. To simulate the movements of the mind, to enhance its dimensionalities, to ease transitions, to create the illusion of atoms and molecules floating. Taking as a basic vocabulary the scientific designations of matter is no different from what Aristotle and Hobbes began with—elemental presences, motion, the observed universe. Whether one chooses to affirm or negate the material world, there is a physical *something* in the experience of beauty—and it is the somethingness of thought and perception, the palpable matrix, that provides the diction for discourse and the vehicle for metaphors here. Poetry, like science, is a way of knowing. The poem: an epistemological artifact, a musicalized synthesis, a layered history of ideas. A thinking dream.

Principles

Matter/language appears.
Equivalences. Form in
gravities of nearness,

emptiness and
knowing as
movable barriers,
each frame a
mantra.

1

Space   /Time's

word/
nothingness

anti/light
anti/dark

twitching
into
rhyme

there   as here

(metals
with albedo
of tar)

after   as before

(creation's
body formed in glistening
dew)

syntax/   mind/
  a wave   a center

the book of surfaces
the book of thou

infinity
parsed
and
fitted to motion
like
the socket
a femur turns
in   the icy wetness
between this/that
glacier/sea's
filled
basin   the round
eye
a shuddering
sphere that wobbles in
gravity's
vacuole
a half-determined
thing   like the origin
of birds   the crawl
of lizards   ichthyoid lips
on pebbles   finned
fingers slipping back into
Urschleim
as if the land said
be
as if sound
swept
into a cry
that became
the thorax

watery
        resemblances in amblystoma
                        and spiny
        dogfish   jaws
                        beginning beneath orbital
                openings

lungs once
gas bladders in carp and
                sea drum   small
                openings become hearing in
                shad's
        contrived bones bridging
water/air and ear

where
        cells could be

                        shark
                        lizard
                        pigeon
        human

        the yolk
an embryo feeds on
                        just a certain
                magnitude
                of star

                        2

What then
or who
                        known as the content of a
                        photo is known

by degrees of
chiaroscuro

the edge of a lawnchair
obscured by the shadow
of elms   a self seen
only when it no longer
exists

dawn's
probability
defined in all
directions   an empty
eyeglass case that snaps
shut   you and
I

a blankness

twisted like the damp
dish towel
pulled through the handle of the
refrigerator
door   whatever we
are
in
the average myth of the average
day   though
half-moons
of fingernails
pull the tide closer
cries of bluejays
strip the needles from fir trees
metaphor/
emptiness and
appetite the function of
equivalence   a cabbage leaf become retina

                    a goat's raw interior the enamel
                    of fangs   ecstasy
                    in dying differences   clitoral
                    firmness   skin or cortex
                    a boundary that breaks
                    apart   where singleness
                    cannot survive

one's room a volume
of motion   color   shape

                    doorknobs
                    from Limoge

                    a scent arising from indoor
                    hyacinth
     February
in the picture window's
downward thrust of icicles
a halted direction   in memory's
              fluency   where the past implodes
                              where a boy sings basso profundo

          as if music
          inhered in coldness

          as if reality
          were the blue remainder of light
          not fully absorbed

          regret
          the momentary warp of space
          between breached atoms of a ballpoint
          pen and the girl writing of her trip to
          Stuttgart   an historic
          snowy winter

place

    an approximate
      freezing   an absolute fabric
                held like zero between the
                teeth   between breaths
                in this room

   the wallpaper's
   floral patterns   needlework sunsets
                    and torn beaches

let them harden into the glazed scenes on teacups
let them be framed like last century's drawings
let them show a grain beneath layers of wax
let them gleam

3

Proximity
  itself
determines
shape
      substance
      a reservoir   the curved crystal of a watch
                  refracting
                  the instant of looking
                  because we are
                  looking

                  and one sees shadows escaping
                  objects   Bouton's Econoline
                  pencil six-sided within a yellow sheath
tapered to darkness

imprinting a reverse
pressure against the moving
hand   an observer's script the bland
                    removal of nubs
                that powder to the touch

        and what one describes already rolled to one side
            of a wicker basket containing pears and soft oranges
turning brown
and oblate   what one writes down as here
                the surreal narrative of a button
                on a thread
                strung across the room

                resting whole
                as the bead of an abacus   the punctured
                cutout of the sun   something that arrives
                as if pushed into the line of sight   a young
                girl forced to recite an iambic sonnet
                stammering only where unstressed   only
                where the intake of breath is an atmosphere
                swarming home   and words tumble in no
                particular order   as though a sestet and six
                yellow sides between one's fingers
                accidentally caught at each other in
                passing   a perpetual hiss in the mind
                the high pitch and susurrus
                where resemblance begins
                as error   where a bruised elbow leaning
                on the table is proof of wood's properties
                where manilla folders open and a week's work
                slides to the floor   fluttering   seesawing
                (who could imagine it?   glued backs held together
                repeatable as books?)   and one reaches
                a threshhold that is two rooms at once
                draughts from the open storm door   wisps

of smoke from spilled sugar carbonizing
in the oven   your voice and mine
blended   altered by their actual
meeting   as if what could be heard
had capacity to hear   could reverse
the lines dividing left from right
and we faced north as we faced south
because what we sought flew toward us
from both broken birch and stalwart
pine   small and striped   the size of
chickadee or nuthatch up and down
the oak's ridged bark   what
coincident clasping of front to back
what amazement   your words shaped to mine

     ah   let them
           meet and pass through
           each other

     ah   the taste of
           being twice

           the hard niggle where
           each of us begins

penetrant
as tea
staining one's teeth   lines painted
                  on the Inuit sculpture
                  of a bird   the blue
                           tongue of the

             dead

             all   myriad
             syndromes of the
             real

possessed

and released

and framed
as if figures could abandon
a landscape   as if stone
could slip out of the Inuit
bird   a cause hovering in the air
to be
          and lost
as meanings are
lost   hieroglyphic
                    to the eye
that recedes   to my dry fingertips
that touch the unformed
     where I would have the both of us
seen
          multiplied
perpetual as color
          in our repetitions
dormant for ages to
                    come
shard-selves cutting
into blank walls
where we flatten into profiles
like animal-headed deities

4

Yet they do not
dissolve
                    the bureau
          and clock radio   the embroidered
                              scarf
          where a crackling web
sways   where the horizontal edge
               of yesterday's *Times*
          folds into arachnean

squares   roundness of eyes
                the measuring
          roods
     of another
length   another time
bent to continuous
seeing   the snake plant
tipping out of its watered
soil   a cactus'
segmented arms hanging from a wrought-iron
stand   a cat lounging
in warm indentations of the risen
sleeper   gynomorphic
variations of dawn
and thalassic hymns   the sea
implicit as plumbing in the 21st
Century
                when the flying
buttresses
of Notre Dame
will yet
hold in the sides of
tomorrow's ex-
pansions   human mimesis
the architecture of vaulted
misery   the great curve

and one awakes in overheated
rooms   sudorific   banal   slightly
amused by the names for
emptiness   February   the mass
of photons   the orotund economies
of nations   the closing distance
between forefinger and
thumb   how intent becomes
grasp   how body shivers itself
into a constant

and momentary
nescience
becomes
interior
  sky

                    a

                        center
                    moves from
                    silence

                                    wall
                            flows

                    a ceiling
                    throbs   all flatness
                    sentient   undulant
                    where a metal ruler
                    would rise and fall
                    on surfaces of the metrical world
and blood form a barrier
at the brain   blood sing
                        like ceaseless
                        rain
into an upturned
skull   blood fill
                    the site of quondam
                    hearing   whimsical
                melodious   requisite
                    as molecules   hollow
            to air   forbidding
            surfeit where the mind moves
            equations   the ratio of wind
            to earth's
        velocity   blood the dark matter
        caught in ventricles   the missing
        whoosh   when once there was more than

— 12 —

height/width/depth   a nanosecond's
eleven dimensions that were all that could ever
be   here played back and
                slow   here the continuous
        Om

Physics

Force and motion.
Number as a web.
Place: the quantum
pulse of probabilities.
Time: two selves
at once.

1

How far without wave or shore
  the dolphin leaping into the squeal and gibber
of mammalian
  tones
          the curved lip
and smooth horizon
    dipping below the eye like acrylic scenes on the bow
of a ship

how far without the albatross rocking on its bosom
  the long curve of its beak
    parallel with the sea and pointed toward inherited
salt

    will a sound carry
  within it the heft of pebbles
or the crab
    upended by the tide

  blown
      sand
honing the voice smooth

         one's throat
a dark portal

    sound the semblance
of
   inland mist rising from lakes

a giant tortoise moving its cracked-skin head
into a hole in space

              its slow heart
beating within sun-locked webbings of air

              breath a transparent speech

nothing in itself

                          2

      the same
                      law
about

          people at the beach

particles within gas clouds

          the configuration of shale
or red blood cells

the tentacles of this galaxy
whirling
about the core of an always spinning
gravity
          a whiplash taking light years
to snap free within a soundless darkness
that is curved
and rippled like a fabric almost pulled taut
by the presence
                  of crowds

each pinpoint
and charged thread
crackling

       with proximity

     everything
touching

      though invisible
    and without dimension   though the eye

is a recent invention
of some blind intent   in the gathered dust

that glows

3

and if only motion exists

              gases furled
like sutures
      stitching lungs

    time the curve
away from fullness

         away from stillness

(the pistil of nicotiana
enclosed by raspberry petals in the June sun

in the solstice
        glare increased
by distance)

at once here and there

                      time

   moving
its heart
     toward a fluid equator
where wholeness
   is the motion
in all things

        where the body
   stiffens in the momentary
hiatus
between breathing in and out

                   impulse
and inertia
the twitch
   of a process
like molecular muscle in steel

    the bridge over the Hudson only a contained movement
within shafts
and cables
         all traffic
a duplication
      and stream
of the memories of matter

pulsing in the rhythm

that is place

4

upright suddenly

the yawp
of blood
that narrow motion
so twisted in extremes
the capillaries of breath
throb
with identity

opening
hyaline corridors
one shouts in
like a child
whose team
has won

feeling the first swell of nipples

space throbbing with emptiness
that we fill with furious
maneuvers

lovers
with arms undulating
in the reach

of galaxies

in dilation
and desire
a woman narrating to the moon

men ejaculating
stars
the great blastula
and fist
closing on us
who wake
to joy
and exhalation

5

now
we
come to it
as to a wall
something rough
and symmetrical

the left hand
transposed
and reaching
through
the right
side of a cupboard
from
childhood

when beds beneath us
were under

and the moon rose above
the wooded curve of the horizon

               one's dream
               not of flying
but of being
       in two rooms at once
waving
to guests
       who enter the walled
interior
we have already
             left

6

constant
change
             in this pond
          the growth
of weeds
                    sunlight seeping through an undisturbed
                    depth
bullfrogs
swelling on the rocks
   their deep voice
belched
from a turbid
             loneliness

and the tadpoles
     almost have feet
             pausing on
             an ancient slide of moraine

awkward adolescents
    bodies too round
too plump
     for such long thin tails

           movements like hips
         without vertical torsos
                   cross sections
of a truncated spine
   seeking
unity
         scattered
by the movement away from us on the rims
     of expanding circles

our shuffling into silt
            our cries at pods brushing
            ankles

the entry of a new force
           rippling
and feculent

         7

something
social

      like stains
     on a white shirt
you didn't see
before you sat
    at this table
    with strangers

                    shame
                            eradicated with good
manners

                    a force
                    exerted by members of a group
                to stay within
it
                            or be repelled

like water on the skin
of new
blueberries

and one is always looking down
at buttons
                    and the spaces
kept shut against
the vectors
of arms unfolding toward

                                        a lover's
                                    buttocks

desire
the motion in silk

                        and the heat of
hurricane lamps
                    at the table
where your eyes gleam
                            and small talk
                            dies

Chemistry

How he enters her
world, transmuting and
contrary, grief
an addition, despair
a possible joy,
insofar as gaining
an electron is called
reduction;

he, allotropic,
more than one
form of substance
in the same physical
state; like water,
being an acid or a base
according to circumstances
in which he finds himself;
disorder and energy
not opposed.

Shifting:

                   his driveway
                  rutted with ice
    the double
         Norway spruce
        leaning
      split trunks in the wind:
          water
                        like the season
sufficient
       and
divided   hardening
   into elements where green
                    combines
                a salt
             with the coldness in his
           voice   as if the brick house
        the red
     and regular crystal
              of
                 an opposing
                       solid
                             burned
               off
like a vapor
                 damp wood
                 hissing
        in the airtight stove

while he watered the almost dry
                    draecena

                              his mood
                         altering
without warning
without a knowledgable drift
                         as though he were a blind skiier being
lifted
      swaying on a hook

                         told of the slope's
condition   imagining the shock to his ankles
                         when he landed

            the shuddering sightless
         downhill run   surface and temperature
                    not of the room he was
      in   then suddenly
                    returned to
                              this trembling in his legs
though he stood still   though he stared at the light
            breaking through gray webbing of the birch tree
   visibly
at least
himself   in this time   the place of his
                    choosing   habiliment in white
            winter's habitual breathless
                    hibernation the illusion
                                   of stasis

and
      upstairs
                    in the red-
            carpeted study
               between shelves
               of Renaissance
            books

redness in the walls
as in tapestries
and doublets of princes

his wife worked on her novel
her typewriter
rearranged the evening
into summer   when a
                                    glass
                    of water
                sweating
        between his hands
                        was a solute
                        warmer
        than darkness
        drawn from wells

when the vertical
blinds of his living room
were not
   the companionable
shadows of stripped
            trees
                        a broken lattice of crystals

                            though
                        the overhead island
                        of sky
        the sunset
                        were now the separable
                        admonitions
                            of an early
                        moon
and the road
worn through its yellow
lines

brought a blackness
                  he could explain
                              as the imprint
                              of an evening
                              without backyard
                              lights   without the acrid
                              air of chimneys

             without a center he exchanged
                    heat
                        from
his wife's sentences
the work
  added to a system
                                    to their marital
                    grid

                     as if separation
                  elongated
the orbit of their
shared
life   and something
              sharp
     assailed
  the outermost
swing
    of his senses

                            (a boy's cry
where ammonia splashed on the bathroom wall
breath seared to the base of his lungs' capacity)

         could he be that young
again   could he
   inhale the same mixture
                       of old porcelain

and damp towels   could he inhibit an
                                    insidious heat
          loss   listening to the sibilance
          of waxed skis

     was he going at such a rate
               down   or towards
whatever loosened into
             time   a
                   never completed
          reaction
so that
he could
     imagine harmonies
               of an old
                   Philco
              where steam knocked
          in silver
       radiators
       and he remembered
     his mother crooning   a noise in his sleep
                           in the walls
              like the mourning of doves

2

But there could be just so much
          heat   if he were himself
                  a
      system
           just so much loss of
    heat   a certain maximum
      death   as if his entropic increase

                   were the fictive need of a fictive past
imagined
                        movement in his standing
still
                             something
                    affixing itself
      in precise measure
to the available niche
          of a quantized
orbit   as if a man weeping
            could not
   hear
   himself
      above the howl of wind   the rattling
                        window pane
         but knew the sound
                    was there
                                a steady static
                         posited
                    (as just now his wife's
          characters
gathered in a parking lot
          sizing each other up

                    he warned himself
               not to get out of the car
               he had so
      furtively
          backed into the darkness beneath
                              a tree   trying
      to emerge
like a subsidiary
walk-on   knowing surely something of himself
            must be there
      their life rushing into each
small silence

                        while she progressed
          through the conflicts
                    of her people   the rising inflection
                            of the woman's voice as she turned
              to her male companion
                              in her old
              Mercedes   the steering just a little
        loose   the man's response sufficiently
          subliminal   so that the plot might
                                        be advanced
when they climbed the rocks above her grandfather's
                              mansion)
and here he was turning
inward   his wife's keys
            clacking like an instrument
counting
isotopes in the medium of his advance
          or backward
    progress   his thoughts colorless and rare

  (the woman pointing to her
                              Mercedes
which was after all   as she explained
          battered
                        saying to the man
    atop an igneous crest   the mansion small
                              so far below
or was it gneiss
or schist   that he mistook her for someone of his
                              own
invention)

      something as astonishing
    as the
    intake
of the lungfish's
            innovative
        breath

                    — 32 —

                as if the boy
                        he once was
                                had exhaled
                                    doubt from his
hearing   as if he now slipped
                        from his dreams
                                like a newly gilled
                        mammal
down the muddy
bank
                        and could measure
                                    the moral
                        volume of

        an
            emptiness
of heart
so easily
occupied   it seemed
wrong
        he should be
happy
                    remembering that job   the white
                                uniform
                the plant behind smokestacks on the shore of a
                                        river
                                where vats swirled and he
                                added
                    caffeine and caramel
                        color
        to darken an invert
sugar   clouding a shifting
clear column
                    the way his mind
                swirled
                now   (what
                                        might the man

be saying as the woman tossed
her hair back with defiant
eroticism   the air soft
in a contrary
landscape of ironwood
and shagbark hickory

what if he himself went upstairs
with tea   the offer of a light
winsome
snack
introducing an unknown
free
energy to a system she was trying to close
without him)

but if her
language
dictated
the exact
temperature
at which reactants
gave up their
natures   then his inward
song
was the hum
drawn up
through a chemist's
hood   issuing
into the air
as toxic
excess
where he wanted facts to be like lock
and key
where he peered through
prisms   an intruder

                    into his own
future   as if instruments
        straightened his lines
   of intent   as if his soul
were the floating
                    disk
                of orange
            light
                        that would not
                            coincide
                        with a paler
                    trembling twin

                            3

Tonight he would be
        glass
            he would flow
    imperceptibly
                        he would be so clear
                        the soft crystals of
                                            self
                    would unlatch
            their closed
facets   would release the infinitessimal
                voltages
        that bound voice to
                an actual
            throat
            as he stepped through the back door
                            the porch light
                    circumscribing
where he stood   not where

                    — 35 —

                    he might walk
not where he might
be within
her hearing
                    not to alter the appearance
          of mansions
    the arrival of
          geese

(not to think
      it was right they should talk of families
                with her girlhood home
in sight   the plot eddying
    that carried them
                away
    the woman tying up her hair
          while that man broke off a branch of the wing tree
      confessing
    there was something in nature he could not
trust
                          as if   she said   you had a
choice)

not where the edge existed
    between freezing and burning   table salt
                              ticking
                on the icy stairs
like the sound of sand
blowing onto a windshield

                        the sound of desert wind
              when
      he had driven so far
          west   in that time
          before they met

(it would seem
sophistical
                    if I said I choose
        to be here   with you

he kicked loose a tussock
of grass
                        and she blushed
he thought
                    ever so faintly)

if there could have been
such a time

                the job
that had almost burned the hands off
an ignorant worker   naphtha and fire
                        what could a man believe
            about water and air   yes
he knew chemicals   and they paid him
            a short bus ride
                an absurd loneliness
            in
            the rubber mask
that protected his eyes
        his breath filtered by the cannister
strapped to his chest
    that allowed him
to function while others emerged
    coughing
                        air force jets
booming through the sound
barrier
                    (everything in nature
        is ours   she said it
with such conviction
                he laughed)

What
even now
     would
   cool his
          gloved
        hands
   so
   quickly
   as the bath of anhydrous
                    ammonia   what would
                           slide
              so easily as water
   from teflon
            explode
   like bars of sodium
   in the sea   *what would*
              survive
solitude
where a train
  whistle
pierced long
  evenings
in Culver City
his boyish letters home
   constructed
   wishfully
as a telluric
  helix
                elements
                    arranged
                in the wistful
        success
   of cylinders   their curves
and extensions
              his love of separations
                 like discredited

— 38 —

                    numbers
              erased from a chart

periodic
    as friendships

            as the appearance of palm trees

                        the gleam
                  of sunlight
            on the black hood
of an old
      Dodge with
      stiff steering

      his progress down
Sepulveda
Blvd   *himself ridiculing*
                    the time devoted to
                Werther's sorrows
          an Indonesian worker
showing him
scars from a Japanese
            bayonet   all these semi-
                  colloids

of his
perception   semen of unknown
                        and un-
                        founded
attractions   as if love
                could be learned

        from
      the kindness
in a
        voice   from the landlord's
                        wife
                who visited his green
                cottage

                          — 39 —

4

And now
the floodlight
like an alien
        sun   so far
            from that time
  it seemed not to reveal huge fir trees
each side of the driveway
                     a star
      of the smallest magnitude
      combusting
his past   his shadow
      thrown on gravel frozen
into ruts   where he turned
      to confront
        a coldness
     in himself   as if long
chains of carbon
  an endless series of hydrogen
    bonds   culminated
    in the low temperatures at which the self
became a superfluid
        oozing through microscopic
flaws
      his reasons
    for apartness
    a slow
unlikely burning
without heat   as if he could ignite like water
     in fluorine gas
like asbestos
like glass   a skin dissolving
from which he stepped

                                              out
            of himself
entirely   her typing
     the most natural
                         sound
                              in the lit stillness

     (the man and woman returned
                    months later to the same
hill   his hangdog look
evidence of what he had argued so vehemently
against in her
               though he refused to call it
conscience   what then
                     what then
she demanded   his loyalty
                              decidedly not
                    the issue
though a war was on   though a priceless tapestry
          had disappeared   and she
stopped short of embracing him
       because   )

these variables
then
   would always
matter: where he was
          and with what need
          his mind
   traveled
            to what other place
               what fever brought new
conductivity to his
blood

                    — 41 —

What metalloid
barely re-
active
harmonies
filled the slanted
space
between
the noise of the woman next door
and news of illness
three thousand
miles away   three lifetimes
removed along the equator that was
like a thin strand
of uncoiled
genetic
material   a dark sliver or shadow
between hemispheres   as if voice could be ductile
and reflective
could dissolve
in the Mississippi
or Colorado
Rivers
to arrive
basic
as floating
oxides   the text
of his mother's
letter
like a newspaper
held over
flame   beginning to brown
in his
thoughts   an application
of heat he had harbored
like style
heaviness

impediment
in the construction
of foreign
  syllables   *as in humid evenings*
                   as in the call
of flamboyant
  screeching birds

                              (because even in his response
there would be implicit
   rejection   and she feared
                   something ulterior with so much
                                     money involved
          or was it power
   he sought   his attitude as he lay back
                                 on withered grass
       suggesting neither lassitude
nor cunning   she almost
                              relented)

What his mother described
        in her graceful script
   not reversible
                nor could there be less
passion for disorder
even in someone as controlled
as he   his life a sudden phosphorous
                        flaring
        alchemical   as if from dried
                   urine and sand
          a simple beat
could produce light   a version
                of integrity

                              (the typing ceased
        her shadow
          moving
across the drawn shade   her voice
calling down   so that he
                    heard her just as he was
entering the cellar
                              and shouted where he
was)

He
had been able to reconstruct
the scene from her
sentences

                                   the indoor
              lighting and
                              discoloration
              of his father's
                                   embalmed
hand   *that spot*
                    showing through cosmetic
                    clay   the deep oxidation
of chemical
hunger   *the sunken tissue*
                              around the closed
        eyes   *the hair arranged*
                                        to conceal
                    sutures and re-
                              arrangements
                    the fracture
                    of organs
    death
neatly laid out
in ruffles   the polished handles

from which a grasp would slide
back toward daylight
the dull
progress
that would continue
in the ground   where the body yields
its metals
where the movement down
toward increased
malleability
in
an
undiscovered
copper
is the slow
accretion
of freed elements
at decay's
electrode   as if a son's
reduction
and crumbling
anger
his refusal to appear at a nonevent
were not loss
but the gain of new
negatives   the undoing
of habitual
affirmations   where motion
is the random song
of ions   his blood
a solvent
for
compounds
of
language
the long night

                                    a potential
          disharmony   a loosening darkness

                          dawn
      a storm of particles   brightening the surface
                                    of ordinary
                                    chromes
                          in toasters
the legs of formica tables
                              decorative strips on the doors of old
                                              Buicks
                    rings of looseleaf binders

      a nimbus
seen around

                    cups
    and the small
    heads
          of
    chickadees
                          so that he could have been going
                                              blind
                                he could have
                          summed
      himself
                into the
                      space
                between
                  protons and
                              neutrons   perfectly
                                    miming
                      the nothing
                      that is
                matter

                        — 46 —

5

"What are you doing?"
                          the kitchen
so bright he put his hands to his
eyes   she hugged
him   "Your ears are so
        cold!"
    He grinned
                      he kept grinning
and
she yelped
when he rubbed his chin's
                  stubbly chill
        into her neck
and he apologized and made
    tea
                              they
                      talked
    her last
chapter would be   perhaps
                                          a
                      marriage
of some kind
                      did he like that
conclusion?
                      he wanted to explain
            himself
    as a habit
      of surface
                      liable
to evaporation
                      how the pressure of light
                      her mere
                  walking
    toward the door

                    was
                        an affair
                    of motion in the cosm
mirroring
                        a joy
                                new
conversions of loss
                    the union
                            of her
            art with
            his random
edges
            where solids would
                    flow   where the transformation
                        of never empty
                    or shapeless
                            space
                                    would be the working
                of a mouth
                                        his fingertips
                        scarred from acids
                    leaving criss-crossed
                        whorls
                    in contact
                            with
                    her smooth arm

did he like that idea?
                                    Oh
                she was so
total   he said
and they talked
                while the plum
brandy
    slurred its way
home   while she
        grew sleepy

                his emergence
            from the kitchen
            after
        she went
upstairs to bed   saying
            don't be long

                    the impossible release of mass
                                    and energy
                                    from a closed
                                    system
                    the triggering
                            enzymes of his sight
                                    nothing
                                to why he turned
                                            his head
                                    upward to the
                            stars arranged like clarities
                            like isolate
                    qualities
of cold and attraction

                            why
                                on the downward slope
                                        of Dogwood Lane
            as he walked between the plowed ridges
                                of the road
                the southern
                        border of his
                land
        he knew the rhythmic
                        gravity

                    of her
breathing
                              of her fluttering eyelids
                    of her sleep-
                              worn syllables
          shaping his name
                                        miraculously

Planets

*Divided into terrene
and Jovian bodies
arranged in order
from the sun.*

I

What spin
what speed
what lack of darkness

                                    Mercury's
                           sifted
                  ground
                     disgorging
          no thirst
where dead
      volcanos
mirror the moon
  or Mars
                       a scorched
                       constancy

                  a slow
                    slough of retrograde
                     noon
             where human eyes
             would twist
                 beneath layers
                   of lids

            where sight
              would be
   the penumbra
      of exfoliate
      stone

                    the heard
            gray margin
                    of chipped
            shadow
                            if the right seed
    arrived
                    a semblance
    cast adrift
from the dust-
                    mirror of a dead planet's wake

        if live oaks
    without
            draperies
    of Spanish moss
reached thinly
        in silvery
        replicas of
        night

                                    and hunger
                            in looking
                                    in helium
                            rain
                    were the exhausted
                    mouthing of a dance
                            the memory of bleached
                        gyrations
                                    in Space
                    as in a window

        if someone arrived
        on a Möbius
            curve
                twisting
        into
    the time-

                    dream of
                    helical
                    pathways
                                        rhythmic chains
                                        of noise
                                        falling from sky

        clashing
        like phonemes

                                            if there were
                                inertial
                                intent enough
                                from human
                                sound
        to disturb the backward motion
                                        of the sun

                            *   *   *

"*Cynthiae figuras
            aemulatur mater
amorum*"
                                        in the pressure of Venus

            the
            soul
            a crushed
                        lens
                beneath speeding
        yellow
                clouds
                                    a skin
                            slipped loose

                            — 54 —

who would not be aghast
                on smooth
                hot plains
who would not abandon words
            where vision curves at land's edge
light
        doubling back
where metals
        melt
    and rubble in shadow
glows red

                the high continent of Ishtar
    the plateau of Lakshmi
a white ring the zero meridian called Eve

fabled
        arrays of women
with lions
and owls
        escaped from the desert

            handed down
    from the feracious
heavens
                        held constant
            from the sun
                            turned so gradually
                    in such a circle
that the follies of our myths
    would be crucibles
    where bones dissolve
                                joy
                the grave admixture of song with sulfur
                where body disappears

lungs blow to cinders

*　　*　　*

but Earth's
   iron
   could be a taste
from the core
          beneath
  tongues
too molten for words
                a history
        of the possible
      in layered light
        where seas flow onto fields of dust
ardor
and fury
    the rhetoric of salt
rising in dawn's redness

   blood of first speech
       before the larynx
presses its tidal bulge toward the moon
    and
moving air
   becomes
  the mantle of rotation

              before cloud and ground
become the image of trees
  in lakes
      pursued
    by what flies between
                 what gasps
        to break
        a vegetable
      surface

                    where mind
      is
the first space
between irregular
crystals
                              a vacancy
                  urging outward

risen free
      of exteriors

                                    an inner
                  drawn to an outer

         such
      escaped
inherence
it must be surrounded
      by skin
by xylem
      by moist
integuments
                     or collapse
            into hyaline negatives

                                 not to confirm the constancy
                        of motion
but the outermost edge
of zero
                  the shape
      where gas
flares into a twisting column
of fire
                     blackening the forest

bringing cold magma
back to igneous and outraged
identity

                        *   *   *

and what would hands do
            with
        red dust

                        the CO$_2$
                        winds of
                        Mars

                                    such thin air
that tornadoes
        blow without force
    breath
        breaking its edge
                        in clouds of dry ice
                            over the polar cap
        desert without
ozone
                            where the Babylonians knew
                                    that
                        invisible
                    pounding
                    from the sun
                                    the ultraviolet
                                            tides
                            lapping ravines
        could be a god's
anger
            the speechless
                    voice of Nergal

only through
　　their own
　　　　suffocating
midnight
　　wakenings
　　　　　　　　and the polygonal
　　　　　　risings
　　　　　　of salt
　　　　　　　from a dead
　　　core
　　the ancient rust
like Earth's dyed
　　caliche
　　　　here without sand
　　a gouged surface

　Phobos
　the moon
appearing twice a day

　　　roaming the landscape like a messenger

　　　　　　its twin
　　　　　Deimos
　　the eye of terror
where blood
　　is
　　a spilled
　　　　　ocher
　　　　　　drying
　　　　　in tracks of the god's
　　　　　　　　chariot
　　　as if life
had gone underground
　　　　　　　　soaked into
　　　　　the rainless furrows

                              and we fell
                        through this
                        horizon
          with nowhere to settle the drift of our lives

prior waterways a dream

                              II

                        Huge ovum
glowing unborn
                                        Jupiter
                    like a sun
              manqué
                                   made liquid

                        its great
red spot a millennial
                    whirlpool

                              as if the motion
        in its
        sea of hydrogen
                    were the current of bodies
              oozing through a membrane
into digestion

                                   so cold
                        if entered
                    our ankles would crack
                        like hot
              porcelain

                              — 60 —

        while the Galilean moons
           persist
Io
     bursts its molten bubos
                    Ganymede
             grooved with ice

      the pockmarked
Europa
  floating dead
     in its tedious
ellipse
                  what if Jupiter
          had fused itself
       into light
      if gravity had spun
         fragments into
         a balled furnace

                its heat
         melting
           frozen
      plains

asteroids crashing toward magnetic maelstroms

     what if consciousness
  was ours
    without this present
plasm
and form
         neither protein
      nor carbon
         fluxion

without marrow
        without organic
perimeter

        our vision
                no more
        than a shifting
of fluids
        east or west

                Mars oblate between two suns

        our moon's face
invisible
        as we streamed in the burning sky

                *   *   *

                        could we then
                enumerate
        the seventeen
                icy bodies
                of Saturn?

        the whirling
                rings
                        the ancients'
                farthest
                edge
        like Time
        seen edge-on
        suddenly
a thread hauling the planet

                    the sea
             on satellite
                    Titan
           cold and
       methane

          in its mid-
     day
             and laggard
     glint
               heaving
     to rhythms
     as regular as
               1 a.m. tides
               along
               the California
               coast

all motion
     shared
        to
     mobilize
        dawn
and dusk

          though a balance everywhere centric
as if Enceladus
          gave back
its fivefold
     reflected white
               as a parallel
to solar
     flame   as if two shepherding bodies
               exchanged
                    orbits
                         to be the tensive gravity
always of a third

*   *   *

```
            so
    slow
            about the sun
                                        so far
            in its blue-green
    banded
            barré
    regions
                                large
                                Uranus
                                in its hot
                        ocean that will not boil
                                yet
                                    so weightless
                        it would drift above Earth's
                                seas
                                    a colored reflection
                        of the moon
                    swelling
            toward the greater
                    gravity
                    of a wobbling
                    core
                                        its lurid
                                    rotation
                            on its
                    side
                                its pink-
                            hued
                            pole
                    and circling
                            plumes
                    nothing but
```

a silence
in which travelers
would dream the humid
forests
of Oberon and Titania

phantom fritillaries at their lips

*   *   *

and if Neptune
were
solid
if it could be
rubbed like amber

swirl
with electricity

if it drew to itself
particles of cosmic
straw
Neptune would still

remain
dim

telescopes would still

search
skies
over the Grand Canyon
for calculable
accumulations of a
self

electro-
　　magnetic waves
　　　symmetrical
　　as the whorls
　　　of a conch　　　inevitable
　　　　　　in smallness
　　　　as the dance
　　　　　of iron filings
　　　toward a child's
　　　　　magnet

a cold sphere predicted
　　　　like the crackling of silk on glass
　　　　　　an equatorial
　　　　　tugging
　　　　known before its shape
　　　　　could be
　　　　　　seen
rippling
　　　the dark solar sea

　　　　　　*　　*　　*

　　so
　　there is presence
　　　perceived
as delay
　　　　　the warp of momentum

　　　　the
　　signature
　　of a witness
　　　　　who does not
　　　appear

Pluto

drawn into orbit

a tenebrous
tracing
for someone to see

where encroachment
occurs
in the stippling
of shadow
a body
once made upon a body

as if mass
as if volume
as if velocity
were three sides of a moving
frame
that approached us

as if we shed the weakness of our force
in revolving
mirrors
where the voice drains
where the past
spreads
in the web between fingers
like a colorless
mold

nothing relative
as oak

                sturdy
                        as the grasp
                                of speech
                        or song

                                the slow
                        swirl
                out there
                        of coldness
                like a net
                                where
there must be Planet X

because a moon
        rolls the wrong
                        way   asteroids
attract
                        beads of water
cling to a glass

                                        because
                        gyroscopes
                        would fly
                        apart

Pluto slam into Neptune

        anticipation
halt the action
                of a lover's
                hand
        raising a cup
                                        where
there is stillness
                in matter

in the motion
        of need

          microgravity
      in membranes
           along the optic
        nerve
    drawn
    to what travels a galactic curve
            like soot

        the unsettled
aphotic
dust

      hunger in the darkness of sleep

Biology

How pairs conspire.
Continuities, places,
dialects, arranged as a
helix.   How parts repeat
themselves.   How appetite
selects.

1

There is only this
steel bridge rusted out

fishermen's
flat-bottomed
boats upended
on a muddy slope   swans congregating
on Muscoot reservoir
the western hill
you call your mountain

this overcast
day's
blank
Pepsico
building
squaring off a rounded
shoreline   stone and glass
supplanting
trees
stripped of bark by white-tail
deer   there is only
our blood
converging   our mixed
inheritance of dirt from Irish
farms
the fields of Krk   eons of insensate
stone
angular unconformities
of Being
imitating granite and
basalt   heaved

                    into a dream of
                              Adriatic air

we are
here   we are here
in the smallest fold
                    of unborn
                         leaves

                    turning off the road
                    behind our house
watching a haggard hawk
                         swoop to her
                         survival

a wound occurring
among pines
               in there the small
     scream   the sudden
                         death

                    the cud
               of a violent cosmos
                    spewed into the eventual
                         coolness of a peony's
               interior
                         the scarlet peony here
                         simply to be here
                    again   as the yellow
                                   finch is here
                         on our wide-mesh fence
                              that protects New Guinea impatiens
                    from the dog   the finch
                              here above the hidden
                                   blackness of the cat
                                   in the cool hostas

                    — 73 —

                    the finch singing
where I dig up plantain
                    from the driveway

                                   where sparrows scour
         the naked stone
for seed   dandelions rooted between
                       broken cinder blocks
                              and brick   the beige
                    spider suddenly the exact color
                       we have painted
                              our garage
         the finch and his
         mate   flying the curve of a sine wave
              up
         into the storm-broken
         branch of a maple   into

                                             opportunity

                    above the cat
                    and spider

2

Opposite Daufuskie Island

                                   Calibogue
                                   Sound yields
                    to the open sea

                                   exhausted
         where we harvest
            a low tide's
               display

                              the sea cucumber opening
                              her tentacles
                                   in the plastic cup we fill
                              with water
            sister to the hydra

                    listen
        listen   we might
                                amble in the twilight
                        on jointed legs
    our skeletons external   turning knee-deep
                                in the shallows of the sand bar
                    we might radiate a more exact
        symmetry   extrude a pharynx
                                in the long wash of sunset

                            our tanned
                        faces uplifted
                        to receive the shadows
                        of pelicans
    the bony parts
    and the soft parts   in the green capacity
                            of sea lettuce   making
                                    selves from
                                    light and the salty
                                secretions of coral
                            and the bequeathed movement of the first
                                alga into a puddle
                            that dried into land
                                    where we might have been
                            blue-green
                            or brown or red

            plants
        hungry for the touch
                    of beetle legs
                    on trigger hairs
        snapping shut spiny lobes
        while we slowly digest
                    death and grow
                    alert to the purposes
                    of hardness   the long projection
                            of the horseshoe crab's
                                    spine

                    — 75 —

        like a weapon

               a deadly dart

  that we see it
  dig
into the
  sand to
  upright itself

                       its carapace later
                       a thin
                  crackling papyrus
                  in the dog's jaws

what would we do clinging and sedentary in a moist habitat
what would we think facing each other across minute distances
like the barely distinguishable parts of moss or the chipped
pine cone that has come to rest beneath pink and yellow zinnias

what amphibian lurch of the backbone takes us into the compost
where the tortoise lays her eggs and the small cadavers of
toads have been flung by the mower's blades what would we assert as
ours as desire is ours as the distinct cavity of the mouth is ours

3

        We have come

to this
particular
  strip
  of Sea Pines Plantation

                  not to forget the twin
                  bridges into Charleston
                  and the fright of traveling
                  thin steel over so much
                  harbor

              not to forget the ladies
                weaving sweet

grass into baskets
among cut flowers
in front of a circular
church

not to be able to say
a Gullah sentence and
know nothing of black women
who live by quick twinings of their fingers
who walk on sand
between washed-up
reeds and razor-sharp
burrs   carrying life
on the surface of pain

not to believe the blind
life of plants
could be
unthinkingly

ours

not to be
automatic
as filter-feeding
mosquito larvae
beating a current
into their
gullets

the earthworm
grinding particles
in its gizzard
not to know
the backward-curved teeth of the snake
holding down what is already a bulge in the body
though everywhere
a need to take
within

to have out-there

                  become

             where will begins
             as the hunger of oxygen
   entering blood   *whispering*
               through the spiracles
                  of grasshoppers
           into the stomata of shade-loving
  trees
        the action of any orifice
    a sentience   *a decision*
          selection a kind of
      pleasure
in momentum

          the way we drove
          to Bogue Island
          and watched the lightning's
          jagged plunge
          sever the sky
          to make our flooded
          route rich in ozone
felt it entering
     our pores
  when we parked at Starvin' Marvin's
           letting the sky carry its load
           of darkness south from Hatteras
     as if there had to be just so much
     of it out there in the distance
     to shade the cornfields
to move us closer
to each other   to balance
         light and salt
         in the clear lymph
         that flows
      between the heart's
     pulse and the first
entry of something

               — 78 —

into a wound   that was the sky
                                        itself
                        that was the white-capped water of Atlantic
                        Beach
and the next day's clear weather
through Emerald Isle   the gouged woods
                                        where condominiums
                        proliferated
                                        like organisms

and we talked of sulfur dioxide
used to kill the wild yeasts
that spoil wine   we sang our road
                                        songs
                spilled the last coffee
                        from a broken thermos

        felt the air
moving against us
                        twisting through the vents
                        sliding along the outer
                                surface of our
                                        human
                volume

                        4

                Home
here it is
home   tiered slope of orange cosmos and white phlox
again   again
    the swollen pods of sweet
                        william   long-necked
                                succulents   low-lying

                                              blue
                       ageratum along the slate walk

                                        nothing
nothing
calls in dialect
so truly
as the wood thrush
                    marking his particular
            tree
            his thin border
         like our
Dogwood Lane between
a neighbor revving
his open-throated
Trans-Am and me
hurtling on the tractor
downhill behind the peach trees
            all this roaring
each side of a street   all this singing
                             from the mulberry tree struggling up
                         between Douglas firs

            all this counterpoint
of bird and bird
                                magnolia and mimosa
                    the separate tangles
                        of caged harmonies   of blown
blossoms and just emerging puffs
of scarlet   up there in the mimosa something like
sea anemones   the hummingbird darting across her
                                habitat
                        into the dilated dusk
                        of our eyes

where the Japanese beetles fall into a plastic bag
duped by synthetic mating scent   by the pheromone
                        that brings them
            copulating in the peach-colored roses
                    where I pluck them in pairs
                        crack them between thumb
                                and forefinger
                in this August
            afternoon
        when I would seek the ants that
            stroke aphids
                    to milk for their
                                honeydew

I would see the round dance
        and the waggle dance
                    of bees   I would tell you
                                just how distant
                        our food is from the hive
                            how many meters
                    my instinct travels
                        to attract
                            your
                        touch
            where you tie up
                    wandering
        morning-
glory's
        mauve trumpets

AFTERWORD

Doing science, unlike *doing* art, music, or poetry, is not commonly associated with beauty. To be sure, the practice of scientific discovery itself is infused with emotion, despite the customary refusal of scientific reports to acknowledge it; and Nature, that awesome agglomerate which surrounds and includes us, and which scientists are devoted to understanding in its particulars, is unarguably the ultimate inspirational wellspring of all the Arts. In *Curve Away from Stillness,* John Allman's love poems sing of a one-ness of art and science as though to weld these distinguishable words and worlds into an indistiguishable all. We are not hearing here poems *about* science. Rather, we listen and inhale Allman's universal language of living, filtered through linguistic allusions to physics, chemistry, and biology as enhancements to the beauty—the poetry—of our lives. I am reminded that Francis Crick, co-discoverer with James Watson of the molecular structure of DNA, wrote a letter to his young son telling about the molecular model of it he and Watson had just constructed. "Our structure is very beautiful," he told his son, reducing, suddenly, one of the great pieces of human scientific discovery to words that universally convey an appreciation of truth's beauty. There is, as Allman tells us, ". . . a physical *something* in the experience of beauty."

Peter S. Coleman
Laboratory of Biochemistry
Department of Biology
New York University

— 83 —

New Directions Paperbooks – A Partial Listing

The Smile at the Foot of the Ladder. NDP386.
  Stand Still Like the Hummingbird. NDP236.
  The Time of the Assassins. NDP115.
Y. Mishima, *Confessions of a Mask.* NDP253.
  Death in Midsummer. NDP215.
Frédéric Mistral, *The Memoirs.* NDP632.
Eugenio Montale, *It Depends.*† NDP507.
  New Poems. NDP410.
  Selected Poems.† NDP193.
Paul Morand, *Fancy Goods/Open All Night.*
  NDP567.
Vladimir Nabokov, *Nikolai Gogol.* NDP78.
  Laughter in the Dark. NDP470.
  The Real Life of Sebastian Knight. NDP432.
P. Neruda, *The Captain's Verses.*† NDP345.
  Residence on Earth.† NDP340.
New Directions in Prose & Poetry (Anthology).
  Available from #17 forward to #52.
Robert Nichols, *Arrival.* NDP437.
  Exile. NDP485. *Garh City.* NDP450.
  Harditts in Sawna. NDP470.
Charles Olson, *Selected Writings.* NDP231.
Toby Olson, *The Life of Jesus.* NDP417.
  Seaview. NDP532.
George Oppen, *Collected Poems.* NDP418.
István Örkeny, *The Flower Show /*
  The Toth Family. NDP536.
Wilfred Owen, *Collected Poems.* NDP210.
José Emilio Pacheco, *Battles in the Desert,* NDP637.
  Selected Poems.† NDP638.
Nicanor Parra, *Antipoems: New & Selected.* NDP603.
Boris Pasternak, *Safe Conduct.* NDP77.
Kenneth Patchen, *Aflame and Afun.* NDP292.
  Because It Is. NDP83.
  Collected Poems. NDP284.
  Hallelujah Anyway. NDP219.
  Selected Poems. NDP160.
Octavio Paz, *Configurations.*† NDP303.
  A Draft of Shadows.† NDP489.
  Eagle or Sun?† NDP422.
  Selected Poems. NDP574.
  A Tree Within.† NDP661.
St. John Perse. *Selected Poems.*† NDP545.
J. A. Porter, *Eelgrass.* NDP438.
Ezra Pound, *ABC of Reading.* NDP89.
  Confucius. NDP285.
  Confucius to Cummings. (Anth.) NDP126.
  Gaudier Brzeska. NDP372.
  Guide to Kulchur. NDP257.
  Literary Essays. NDP250.
  Selected Cantos. NDP304.
  Selected Letters 1907-1941. NDP317.
  Selected Poems. NDP66.
  The Spirit of Romance. NDP266.
  Translations.† (Enlarged Edition) NDP145.
  Women of Trachis. NDP597.
Raymond Queneau, *The Blue Flowers.* NDP595.
  Exercises in Style. NDP513.
  The Sunday of Life. NDP433.
Mary de Rachewiltz, *Ezra Pound.* NDP405.
Raja Rao, *Kanthapura.* NDP224.
Herbert Read, *The Green Child.* NDP208.
P. Reverdy, *Selected Poems.*† NDP346.
Kenneth Rexroth, *Classics Revisited.* NDP621.
  More Classics Revisited, NDP668.
  100 More Poems from the Chinese. NDP308.
  100 More Poems from the Japanese.† NDP420.
  100 Poems from the Chinese. NDP192.
  100 Poems from the Japanese.† NDP147.
  Selected Poems. NDP581.
  Women Poets of China. NDP528.
  Women Poets of Japan. NDP527.
  World Outside the Window, Sel. Essays, NDP639.
Rainer Maria Rilke, *Poems from*
  The Book of Hours. NDP408.
  Possibility of Being. (Poems). NDP436.
  Where Silence Reigns. (Prose). NDP464.
Arthur Rimbaud, *Illuminations.*† NDP56.
  Season in Hell & Drunken Boat.† NDP97.
Edouard Roditi, *Delights of Turkey.* NDP445.

  Oscar Wilde. NDP624.
Jerome Rothenberg, *New Selected Poems.* NDP625.
Nayantara Sahgal, *Rich Like Us,* NDP665.
Saigyo, *Mirror for the Moon.*† NDP465.
Ihara Saikaku, *The Life of an Amorous*
  Woman. NDP270.
St. John of the Cross, *Poems.*† NDP341.
Jean-Paul Sartre, *Nausea.* NDP82.
  The Wall (Intimacy). NDP272.
Delmore Schwartz, *Selected Poems.* NDP241.
  The Ego Is Always at the Wheel, NDP641.
  In Dreams Begin Responsibilities. NDP454.
Stevie Smith, *Collected Poems.* NDP562.
  New Selected Poems, NDP659.
Gary Snyder, *The Back Country.* NDP249.
  The Real Work. NDP499.
  Regarding Wave. NDP306.
  Turtle Island. NDP381.
Enid Starkie, *Rimbaud.* NDP254.
Robert Steiner, *Bathers.* NDP495.
Antonio Tabucchi, *Letter from Casablanca.* NDP620.
Nathaniel Tarn, *Lyrics . . . Bride of God.* NDP391.
Dylan Thomas, *Adventures in the Skin Trade.*
  NDP183.
  A Child's Christmas in Wales. NDP181.
  Collected Poems 1934-1952. NDP316.
  Collected Stories. NDP626.
  Portrait of the Artist as a Young Dog. NDP51.
  Quite Early One Morning. NDP90.
  Under Milk Wood. NDP73.
Tian Wen: *A Chinese Book of Origins.* NDP624.
Lionel Trilling, *E. M. Forster.* NDP189.
Martin Turnell, *Baudelaire.* NDP336.
  Rise of the French Novel. NDP474.
Paul Valéry, *Selected Writings.*† NDP184.
Elio Vittorini, *A Vittorini Omnibus.* NDP366.
Rosmarie Waldrop, *The Reproduction of Profiles,*
  NDP649.
Robert Penn Warren, *At Heaven's Gate.* NDP588.
Vernon Watkins, *Selected Poems.* NDP221.
Weinberger, Eliot, *Works on Paper.* NDP627.
Nathanael West, *Miss Lonelyhearts &*
  Day of the Locust. NDP125.
J. Wheelwright, *Collected Poems.* NDP544.
Tennessee Williams, *Camino Real.* NDP301.
  Cat on a Hot Tin Roof. NDP398.
  Clothes for a Summer Hotel. NDP556.
  The Glass Menagerie. NDP218.
  Hard Candy. NDP225.
  In the Winter of Cities. NDP154.
  A Lovely Sunday for Creve Coeur. NDP497.
  One Arm & Other Stories. NDP237.
  Stopped Rocking. NDP575.
  A Streetcar Named Desire. NDP501.
  Sweet Bird of Youth. NDP409.
  Twenty-Seven Wagons Full of Cotton. NDP217.
  Vieux Carre. NDP482.
William Carlos Williams,
  The Autobiography. NDP223.
  The Buildup. NDP259.
  The Doctor Stories. NDP585.
  Imaginations. NDP329.
  In the American Grain. NDP53.
  In the Money. NDP240.
  Paterson. Complete. NDP152.
  Pictures form Brueghel. NDP118.
  Selected Letters. NDP589.
  Selected Poems (new ed.). NDP602.
  White Mule. NDP226.
  Yes, Mrs. Williams. NDP534.
Yvor Winters, *E. A. Robinson.* NDP326.
Wisdom Books: *Ancient Egyptians.* NDP467.
  Early Buddhists, NDP444; *Forest* (Hindu).
  NDP414; *Spanish Mystics.* NDP442; *St. Francis.*
  NDP477; *Taoists.* NDP509; *Wisdom of the Desert.*
  NDP295; *Zen Masters.* NDP415.

For complete listing request free catalog from
New Directions, 80 Eighth Avenue, New York 10011